JOHN *Tyler*

Our PRESIDENTS

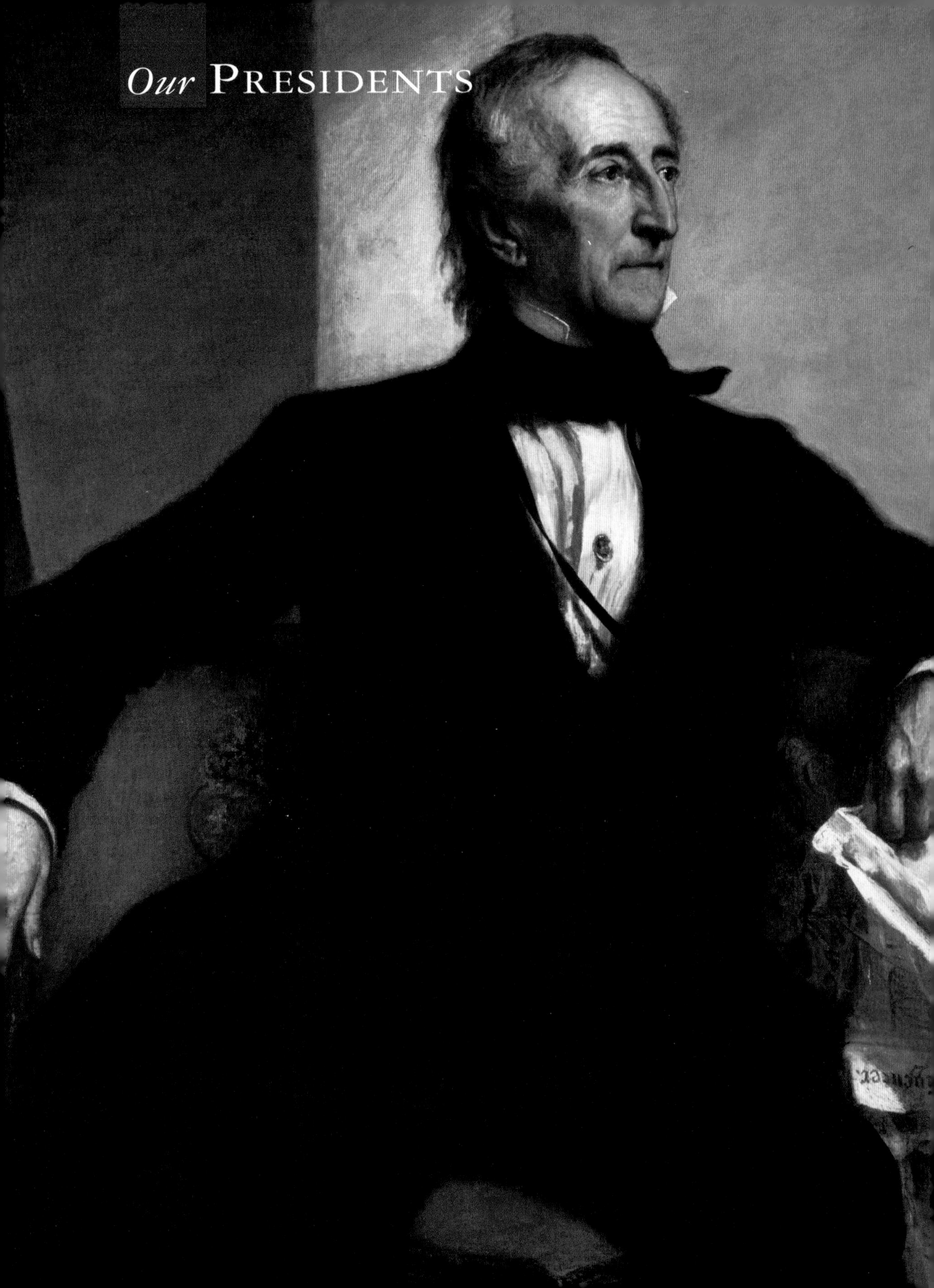

JOHN *Tyler*

OUR TENTH PRESIDENT

By Steven Ferry

SPIRIT
of America™

The Child's World®, Inc.
Chanhassen, Minnesota

8

JOHN *Tyler*

Published in the United States of America by The Child's World®, Inc.
PO Box 326 • Chanhassen, MN 55317-0326 • 800-599-READ • www.childsworld.com

Acknowledgments
The Creative Spark: Mary Francis-DeMarois, Project Director; Elizabeth Sirimarco Budd, Series Editor; Robert Court, Design and Art Direction; Janine Graham, Page Layout; Jennifer Moyers, Production

The Child's World®, Inc.: Mary Berendes, Publishing Director; Red Line Editorial, Fact Research; Cindy Klingel, Curriculum Advisor; Robert Noyed, Historical Advisor

Photos
Cover: White House Collection, courtesy White House Historical Association; Adams National Historical Park: 17; Chicago Historical Society: 36; Corbis: 11, 13, 26, 35; Kevin Davidson: 33; Benjamin Harrison Home, Indianapolis, Indiana: 20, 22, 23; The Hermitage: 19; Library of Congress: 12, 15, 16, 21, 29, 31, 32, 34; National Portrait Gallery, Smithsonian Institution/Art Resource: 24; Sherwood Forest Plantation, Charles City, VA: 7, 8 (©Greg Hadley), 27, 37; Historic Hudson Valley, Tarrytown, New York: 14; courtesy of J. Tyler Griffin and the White House Historical Association: 10; courtesy of the Tyler family: 6; College of William and Mary: 9

Registration
The Child's World®, Inc., Spirit of America™, and their associated logos are the sole property and registered trademarks of The Child's World®, Inc.

Library of Congress Cataloging-in-Publication Data
Ferry, Steven, 1953–
   John Tyler : our tenth president / by Steven Ferry.
      p. cm.
   Includes bibliographical references and index.
   ISBN 1-56766-849-6 (alk. paper)
   1. Tyler, John, 1790–1862—Juvenile literature. 2. Presidents—United States—Biography—
Juvenile literature. [1. Tyler, John, 1790–1862. 2. Presidents.]   I. Title.
   E397 .F47 2001
   973.5'8'092—dc21

                                                      00-010945

16   23   34

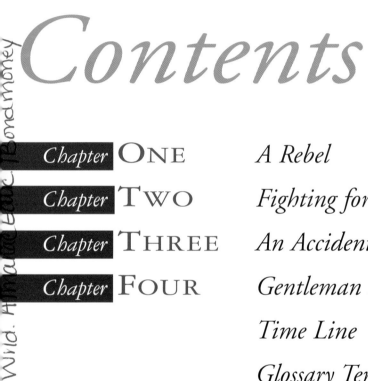

Contents

Chapter ONE

A Rebel

John Tyler was a president with an independent mind. He refused to make decisions based on what others wanted him to do. Unfortunately, this meant that other politicians often refused to cooperate with him.

JOHN TYLER OFTEN SAID HE WAS A DISTANT relative of Wat Tyler, the leader of a peasant revolt against Richard the Second of England. When the king wanted to increase taxes, Wat and his followers led a rebellion, a battle against the English government. But Wat was soon killed, and his rebellion was crushed. Like Wat, who was brave enough to stand up to King Richard, John Tyler was also a brave man. He often stood up for what he believed. Unfortunately, just like Wat, he often lost.

John's great grandfather, Henry Tyler, came to the United States from England in 1653. He settled near Williamsburg, Virginia. The family enjoyed success in their new homeland. By the time John was born on March 29, 1790, they owned a large tobacco farm, called

Interesting Facts

▸ The home where John Tyler was born is still standing, but it is privately owned and closed to the public.

▸ John Tyler lived at Greenway in his youth, but he later bought another Virginia plantation called Sherwood Forest. His family has owned the estate ever since. In fact, Tyler's grandson still lives at the plantation today.

a plantation, that they named Greenway. It was on the James River between Richmond and Williamsburg. The Tylers also owned 40 slaves, who worked hard to run the plantation. John's mother, Mary, died in 1797. After this sad event, his father, Judge John Tyler, lovingly raised John and his seven brothers and sisters.

Judge Tyler was a school friend and admirer of the third American president, Thomas Jefferson. Judge Tyler was an independent man who supported the American Revolution, the war in which the United States won its freedom

Judge Tyler was a respected citizen of Virginia who became the governor of the state in 1809. He taught his son to be independent and to stand up for his beliefs.

from Great Britain. He raised his children to believe firmly in the ideas of the U.S. **Constitution.** He told them exciting tales of the Revolution and the brave patriots who fought for liberty. Judge Tyler was very proud to be an American.

Although John was a gentle person, he led his own rebellion while he was still quite young. His schoolteacher was a strict, unkind man named William McMurdo. He often whipped students who misbehaved, or even those who gave an incorrect answer. John was tired of McMurdo's severe punishments. One day, he and the other schoolchildren knocked McMurdo to the floor, tied him up, and locked the school door behind them as they left. McMurdo lay on the floor all afternoon before a passerby freed him. Judge Tyler did not punish his son. He was proud that John had rebelled against a tyrant, a person who uses his power unfairly.

In 1802, John enrolled in classes at the College of William and Mary in Williamsburg. He studied Latin, Greek, English literature, history, and mathematics before graduating in 1807. He returned home determined to become a lawyer. He also dreamed of a career in **politics.** At the time, young men who wanted to study law did not go to school. Instead, they worked with a lawyer to learn the profession. John studied law with his father and then with his cousin, Samuel Tyler.

When Tyler enrolled at the College of William and Mary, he followed in the footsteps of two great American leaders: Thomas Jefferson and James Monroe.

Letitia Christian and John Tyler were engaged for almost five years before they finally married. Tyler wrote love poems and letters to her. "To ensure your happiness is now my only object," he once wrote, "And whether I float or sink in the stream of fortune, you may be assured of this, that I shall never cease to love you."

One year earlier, John had met Letitia Christian. She was the shy and loving daughter of a wealthy Virginia merchant. John courted Letitia for five years, writing poems and playing the violin for her. He finally kissed her just a few weeks before they married in 1813, on his 23rd birthday.

John Tyler passed his law exams in 1809. The opportunity to begin a career in politics came that same year. Judge Tyler had been elected the governor of Virginia the year before, and John traveled to live with him in the state capital, Richmond. He began working at the law office of Edmund Randolph, who was the first U.S. attorney general while George Washington was president. An attorney general is a lawyer who handles a government's legal affairs.

With Randolph's help, Tyler became involved in politics. By 1811, he was elected to the Virginia state **legislature.** A long career in politics had begun.

John went to live in Richmond after his father became the governor of Virginia. By 1811, John would be working at the state Capitol as a member of the Virginia legislature.

Chapter TWO

Fighting for the Constitution

Tyler began his political career in the Virginia House of Delegates. Later he served many years in Congress, both in the House of Representatives and in the Senate. He was also the governor of Virginia, just as his father had been.

TYLER WAS ACTIVE DURING HIS FIRST FIVE years in the Virginia House of Delegates, which was one part of the state's legislature. He tried to make sure that his fellow lawmakers followed the **principles** of the U.S. Constitution. For one thing, the men who wrote the Constitution wanted to limit the power of the **federal** government. They wanted to give people in the individual states the right to make decisions for themselves. Like many Southerners, Tyler believed that strengthening the federal government would threaten states' rights. Southerners were especially worried that a strong national government would try to outlaw slavery.

Tyler fought federal control of the states in many ways. For one thing, he was against

the Second Bank of the United States. This powerful bank was in charge of the federal government's money. Tyler believed smaller banks in each state should have more control. The U.S. government also had begun giving public land to homesteaders, people who traveled to the **frontier** to build homes and farms. Tyler believed the states should decide how to use their own land. He also was against the federal government giving money to the states. Instead, he believed each state should take care of itself, without accepting federal funds.

The Second Bank of the United States (above) was not a government bank, but a private bank owned by 200 of the richest people in America, as well as some foreigners. These people wanted the U.S. government to put all its money in their bank.

In 1818, the government sent General Andrew Jackson (above) into Georgia to protect U.S. settlers from attacks by Native Americans.

In 1816, Tyler was elected to represent Virginia in the U.S. House of Representatives, which is part of Congress. As a national lawmaker, he continued his battle to uphold the Constitution.

Two years later, in 1818, General Andrew Jackson invaded East Florida, which was then controlled by the Spanish. The government had only given him permission to fight the Seminole Indians in Georgia, who had been attacking American settlers. But Jackson invaded Florida as well. Once there, he and his troops attacked and killed many British and Spanish citizens in the region.

Tyler felt Jackson had done something wrong. He had received no orders from the U.S. government to attack East Florida. The Constitution says that no single person, not even a general or president, has the right to make such a serious decision. Still, Jackson became an American hero because he gained more land for the nation. Tyler spoke out against Jackson. He bravely ignored Jackson's popularity and stood up for what he believed. As always, Tyler felt it was more important to uphold the Constitution than to go along with popular opinions.

In 1820, Congress had to decide whether to allow slavery in new **territories** such as Missouri. Northerners were against expanding slavery into new places. But Southerners were concerned that if it were outlawed in these

After attacking the Seminole Indians, General Jackson and his troops crossed the border into Florida and seized Spanish territory. Jackson did this without orders from the U.S. government, making some people angry. Most Americans were pleased to add new land to the nation, however.

▶ Europeans started the slave trade 300 years before John Tyler was born. By the time this practice was finally stopped, 10 million Africans had been kidnapped and forced into slavery in the New World. Most slaves in the United States worked on Southern cotton or tobacco plantations.

One reason that Tyler stood so firmly by the rights of the individual states was because he was a slaveholder. Like most Southerners, Tyler believed the Constitution allowed Americans to keep slaves and fought any attempt to take away that right. Slavery was not outlawed until after the American Civil War.

areas, the federal government might try to make it illegal in the South as well. Congress created the Missouri **Compromise,** giving both sides part of what they wanted. One part of the Compromise outlawed slavery in all U.S. lands north of a specific point. Tyler voted against the Compromise because it limited the places

where slavery was legal. He believed the Constitution allowed individual states to decide whether to allow it. Most other congressmen disagreed with Tyler, and they passed the Missouri Compromise.

During his time in Congress, Tyler usually cast a losing vote. His lack of success discouraged him. He also suffered from poor health. He caught colds easily and had stomach problems. In 1821, he left Congress, returning home to Virginia.

Tyler was not out of politics for long. Two years later, he was again elected to the Virginia House of Delegates. He served from 1823 to 1825. During the presidential election of 1824, Tyler supported John Quincy Adams, who was running against Andrew Jackson. Adams won the election. But soon after he took office, Tyler realized that the new president wanted to increase the federal government's power. He was disappointed and refused to continue helping him.

In 1825, Tyler was elected governor of Virginia. He spent the next two years trying unsuccessfully to improve education and transportation in the state. At the end of 1826,

Tyler supported John Quincy Adams during the election of 1824. Once Adams entered office, Tyler became unhappy with his actions. For one thing, President Adams wanted the federal government to have more power than the states. He planned to use federal funds to pay for projects in individual states. Adams was also firmly opposed to slavery.

► Throughout his career, Tyler was committed to states' rights. He believed the federal government's powers should be limited to those described in the Constitution.

► In 1838, Letitia Tyler suffered a stroke, which is a serious injury to the brain. It left her unable to walk, and she seldom left her bedroom after that.

Tyler was elected to the U.S. Senate. He headed for Washington the following January and immediately joined the Democratic Party, which was preparing for the next election. This **political party** opposed John Quincy Adams and supported Andrew Jackson. Although Tyler did not fully believe in Jackson's ideas, he felt he was a better choice for president than Adams. For one thing, Jackson was also against the Second Bank of the United States. Many Americans admired Jackson, and he easily won the presidential election of 1828.

Tyler soon came to disagree with President Jackson's plans for the nation. In 1833, Jackson signed the Force **Bill.** This gave the president the power to send federal troops into a state if it refused to obey laws. Tyler believed the bill was **unconstitutional,** but he was the only senator to oppose it. When Jackson removed all U.S. government funds from the Second Bank of the United States, Tyler decided not to support Jackson anymore. Tyler may have disliked the bank, but Jackson acted without the necessary approval from Congress. The Constitution says that the president cannot make such a decision unless Congress agrees to it.

Tyler left the Democratic Party and joined a new political party, the Whigs, who opposed President Jackson. Soon Tyler and other senators decided that Jackson had to be punished. They voted to censure him. When Congress censures the president, its members state formally that they think he has done something wrong. Jackson replied to the censure by saying he did not have to do what the Senate wanted. In 1836, leaders from Virginia ordered their senators to cancel the censure. Tyler refused to do so. He left his position instead. As always, he refused to do something he felt was wrong.

People in Virginia still believed Tyler was a good leader. Two years later, he was reelected to the Virginia House of Delegates. The other lawmakers elected him Speaker of the House in 1839. This meant he took charge of all their meetings.

In 1840, it was time for another election. The Whig Party needed to choose a presidential **candidate,** and they nominated a former war hero from the North named William Henry Harrison. The party chose Tyler to run as vice president, in part because

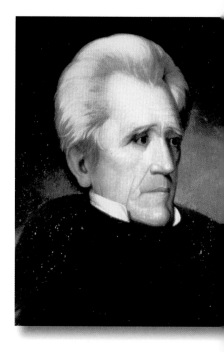

Although Andrew Jackson (above) and Tyler were both Southern Democrats, they did not agree on many issues. Tyler left the Democratic Party and joined the Whigs because he believed Jackson was becoming too powerful.

Interesting Facts

▸ The election of 1840 was not the first time William Henry Harrison ran for president. He lost the election of 1836 to Martin Van Buren, who had been Andrew Jackson's vice president. The Whig Party was disappointed when Van Buren won because he would keep Jackson's policies. They began campaigning for the next election right away and eventually chose John Tyler as the vice presidential candidate. Harrison defeated Van Buren in that election.

he opposed Jackson. They also knew that many Southerners would support Tyler. After all, he was from Virginia and owned slaves. Tyler did not agree with many of the Whigs' ideas, but the party believed he would not create problems as vice president. In December of 1840, William Henry Harrison won the election, and Tyler became vice president.

20

DURING THE ELECTION OF 1840, THE WHIG PARTY RAN WHAT WAS KNOWN AS the "Hard Cider and Log Cabin Campaign." It changed the way elections were run in the United States. In the past, candidates had suggested sensible solutions to the problems the nation faced. This allowed people to decide intelligently how to vote. In 1840, the Whigs decided the best way to win the election was to entertain people and to insult the other candidate.

After the Whigs asked William Henry Harrison to run for president, they worked to create a positive image for him. They praised him as a war hero. To make him seem like a regular person, they said he lived on the frontier in a log cabin. He was really a man from a wealthy family who lived in a riverside mansion. The Whigs said Harrison liked to drink hard cider, which is an alcoholic drink made from apples, instead of expensive wines from foreign countries. They described his opponent, Martin Van Buren, as someone who lived like a king. They said Van Buren didn't understand the needs of the average American. They hoped this would increase Harrison's appeal to ordinary Americans.

Harrison traveled around the country in a wagon. It had a log cabin built on top of it. The wagon also carried a huge barrel of cider. Bands played music while people cheered. The Whigs passed out hard cider for everyone to drink. People chanted slogans such as "Van, Van, is a used-up man!" and "Tippecanoe and Tyler, too!" Tippecanoe was Harrison's nickname after his 1811 victory over the Shawnee Indians at the Battle of Tippecanoe.

Chapter THREE

An Accidental Presidency

William Henry Harrison was the nation's ninth president. He had the misfortune of being the first president to die in office.

TYLER'S WIFE, LETITIA, WAS QUITE ILL WHEN he became vice president. It would have been difficult for her to move to Washington. So Tyler planned to handle his duties from home, as vice presidents had done in the past. He traveled to the nation's capital to attend President Harrison's **inauguration.** The 68-year-old president had ridden on horseback to the Capitol. Then he gave the longest inaugural speech in history. He spoke for more than two hours in the freezing rain. He wore no hat or coat. That evening, Harrison came down with a cold.

The next day, Tyler returned to Virginia. Very soon, President Harrison's cold turned into a serious illness called **pneumonia.** Less than one month after his inauguration,

Harrison lay sick in bed. Tyler had no idea the president was ill. Harrison died on April 4, 1841, but Tyler did not receive word until the next day.

No president had ever died in office before. The Constitution said that the vice president would take over the duties of the president, but it didn't say he actually *became* the president. Americans wondered what would happen next.

William Henry Harrison died on April 4, a month after his inauguration. His presidency was the shortest in American history.

23

Tyler was shocked and saddened to learn that President Harrison was dead. He rushed back to Washington to take on the duties of the president.

Tyler arrived in Washington on April 6. He met Harrison's **cabinet** members, who told him he was only the acting president. This meant he did not have the same powers a president normally would have. They would have to approve all his actions. Tyler said, "I am very glad to have in my cabinet such able **statesmen** as you. But I can never consent to being dictated to as to what I shall or shall not do…. I am the president." He then said if any cabinet member opposed his decisions, he would be asked to give up his position.

Congress agreed with Tyler. It confirmed his presidency on April 9, 1841. But this did not stop many politicians from addressing letters to Tyler as "Acting President" and "Ex-Vice President." Tyler returned all these letters unopened.

Today Americans know there is always a chance the president will die in office. They count on the government to keep working if this happens. Tyler's actions created the tradition that has always been followed when a president dies in the United States. Even so, newspaper reporters and congressmen began calling Tyler "His Accidency" and "The Accidental President." The cabinet refused to support him. Its members had expected to have a great deal of power with Harrison as president. Tyler would not allow this.

The new president had no advisers and no supporters in the government. And soon, he would have no political party. It became clear that Tyler would face many problems when the Whigs in Congress wanted to create another national bank. He **vetoed** both bills introduced on this issue. It was the first of many battles he would fight with Congress.

In an effort to force Tyler out of office, all but one member of the cabinet resigned in the fall of 1841. Tyler replaced them within two days, selecting Democrats for the posts. The Whigs were furious and forced him out of the party. At the same time, the Democrats did

not trust Tyler because he had left their party years before. Most of the cabinet members did not keep their positions very long. During the rest of his presidential term, 22 men filled the six positions in his cabinet.

Without a stable cabinet or support from either party in Congress, Tyler could accomplish few of his goals. The Whigs in Congress even tried to **impeach** him when he vetoed a **tariff** bill in 1842. They grew even angrier when he refused to replace all Democrats in government positions with people from the Whig Party. But Tyler believed in making decisions according to what was best for the nation, not for a political party.

Through these difficulties, Tyler faced problems in his personal life as well. Letitia was confined to a wheelchair in an upstairs room at the White House. She came down only once, to attend the wedding of their daughter, Elizabeth. Letitia died just 17 months after Tyler entered office. Their daughter-in-law, Priscilla Cooper Tyler, acted as the White House hostess until 1844. That year, Tyler married a young woman from New York named Julia Gardiner.

Throughout his presidency, Tyler continued to veto bills with which he did not agree. He opposed bills to create new tariffs and to sell public lands. He vetoed bills until congressmen improved them. But then Congress struck back. Tyler's secretary of the navy began a program to build steam-powered, iron ships. Congress introduced a bill to refuse payment for them. Of course, Tyler vetoed the bill. But then Congress used its power to overrule his veto, and the bill became law. This was the first time Congress successfully united to fight a presidential veto.

Tyler was able to achieve some goals. The "log-cabin" bill allowed people to settle and improve public lands. Then they could purchase 160 acres for their families for a small fee, just $1.25

After Letitia's death, Tyler married Julia Gardiner, a 24-year-old woman from New York. Tyler was 54 at the time, a full 30 years older than Julia. Their small and secretive wedding took place in June of 1844 and surprised the public. Tyler was the first president to get married while in office.

per acre. The Postal Reform Act of 1844 was one of Tyler's biggest successes. It lowered postal rates and added new services. It also recommended the use of the telegraph to send messages. The telegraph was a new invention that sent coded messages through electric wires.

Tyler had some success with foreign affairs, the nation's dealings with other countries. The Webster-Ashburton **Treaty** of 1842 was an agreement that settled the dispute over the boundary between Canada and Maine. The United States was given 7,000 square miles, and the Canadians were given 5,000. Tyler also prevented the British from taking over Hawaii in 1842. He sent a group of advisors to China in 1844. The result was the Treaty of Wang Hiya, which allowed U.S. ships to buy and sell goods in China.

In 1843, Tyler began secret talks with leaders in Texas, which was then an independent country. Many Texans wanted to become a part of the **Union,** and Tyler was in favor of this. He signed a treaty with the president of Texas, Sam Houston. But the U.S. Senate still had to approve it, and it refused to do so at first. For one thing, they did not want President Tyler to take credit for helping the nation grow. Also, the treaty said that slavery would be allowed in Texas, and many Northern senators would not accept this.

As the election of 1844 drew near, neither the Democrats nor the Whigs wanted Tyler to be their presidential candidate. The Democrats chose James Polk, whom most people had never heard of. But Polk promised to help the nation expand across the continent. For one thing, he was very much in favor of the **annexation** of Texas. Americans wanted the nation to spread from coast to coast.

Polk won the election. This showed Congress that the American people were in favor of annexing Texas. Three days before Tyler left office, Texas was admitted to the Union.

Tyler secretly worked with the president of Texas, Sam Houston (above), to create a treaty. Both men wanted Texas to become part of the United States.

JULIA GARDINER WAS THE daughter of a wealthy New York family. The beautiful young woman surprised her friends when she posed as a model for a department store advertisement, shown here. In her hands, she carries a small sign. "I'll purchase at Boger & Mecamly's," it reads. "Their goods are beautiful and astonishingly cheap."

Julia visited Washington, D.C., in 1842, and impressed all of society—including President Tyler. He had just lost his wife and felt lonely. Julia charmed him, and he asked her to marry him. She refused, but an accident changed her mind.

Julia and her father, David Gardiner, were guests of the president on the new steamship, the *Princeton*. It was February 28, 1844. The captain of the ship wanted to show off the Peacemaker, the largest naval gun in the world. The third time it was fired, it exploded and killed Mr. Gardiner. President Tyler and Julia had been below deck and were unharmed.

Tyler helped Julia through the loss of her father. She grew to care for him a great deal, and they married secretly four months later. They had seven children together. Tyler had 15 children in his lifetime.

Mrs. Tyler took over as first lady for the last eight months of her husband's term. She held several lively parties, including one for 3,000 guests. When they returned to live in Virginia, Julia acted as mistress of the plantation until the Civil War. She also raised their many children.

After the war, with her husband long dead, Julia had no money. She asked Congress for help. In 1870, she and Mrs. Mary Lincoln were given $1,200 each. After 1881, this amount was raised to $5,000 for all former first ladies. Julia lived her last eight years comfortably in Richmond and was buried at her husband's side.

Chapter FOUR

Gentleman Farmer

By the end of his term, Tyler was more than ready to leave his "accidental presidency." He and Julia were happy to return to their home in Virginia.

JOHN AND JULIA TYLER WERE HAPPY TO return to Virginia. Tyler said that when he was called to Washington after Harrison's death, "I foresaw that I was called to a bed of thorns. I now leave that bed which has afforded me little rest, and eagerly seek repose in the quiet enjoyments of rural life."

The Tyler's home was a 1,200-acre plantation called Sherwood Forest, which had been built in 1616. It was three miles from Greenway, where he had grown up. He had purchased it from his cousin in 1842 for $12,000. The Tylers named it Sherwood Forest in honor of the English outlaw, Robin Hood, who lived in Sherwood Forest. Tyler saw himself as an outlaw, too, because he refused to do what the political parties expected of him. Tyler added a

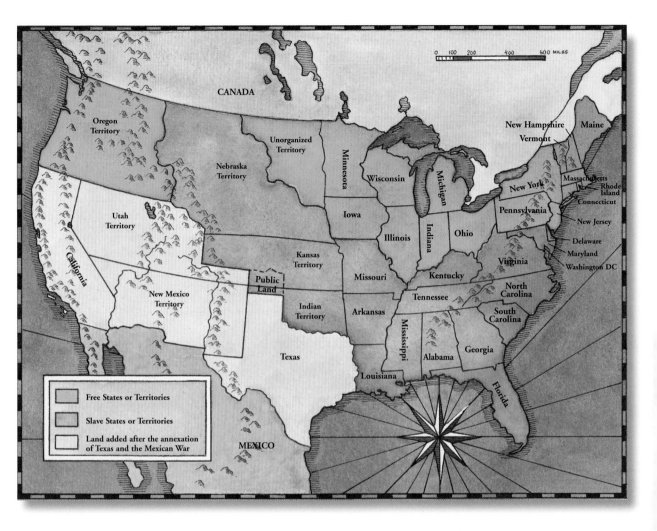

The map includes the following labels: CANADA, Oregon Territory, Unorganized Territory, New Hampshire, Vermont, Maine, Nebraska Territory, Minnesota, Wisconsin, Michigan, New York, Massachusetts, Rhode Island, Connecticut, Utah Territory, Iowa, Pennsylvania, New Jersey, California, Illinois, Indiana, Ohio, Delaware, Maryland, Washington DC, Kansas Territory, Missouri, Kentucky, Virginia, New Mexico Territory, Public Land, Tennessee, North Carolina, Indian Territory, Arkansas, South Carolina, Texas, Mississippi, Alabama, Georgia, Louisiana, Florida, MEXICO

Legend:
- Free States or Territories
- Slave States or Territories
- Land added after the annexation of Texas and the Mexican War

0 100 200 400 600 MILES

ballroom to the mansion so people could dance and enjoy parties at his home. This addition made it the longest wooden-frame house in America.

Tyler spent the next 17 years farming his land. He enjoyed hunting foxes and other wild animals at Sherwood Forest. He played the violin for guests while Julia played the guitar. The family kept many pets and enjoyed their time together. He returned to a peaceful and pleasant existence.

After Tyler left the presidency, the nation grew much larger. During James Polk's presidency, the nation took control of a large portion of the Oregon Territory (shown in green at left). After the Mexican War, the United States grew by nearly 1.2 million square miles. This rapid growth created problems for the country. No one could decide whether the new territories should allow slavery.

*The Civil War began on
April 12, 1861, when the
South fired on Fort Sumter,
a Union fort off the coast of
Charleston, South Carolina.*

Tyler did not leave public life completely. He later rejoined the Democratic Party. In 1860, he became the chancellor of the College of William and Mary, an important leader at the school. Then, in February of 1861, civil war threatened to tear the nation apart. Tyler returned to politics as chairman of the Peace Convention, a special meeting held just before the war began. The convention included people from 21 states, all hoping to find a compromise that would prevent a war. When

As a member of the Con-
federate congress, Tyler
was considered a traitor
by many Americans.

no solution could be found, Tyler recom-
mended that Virginia leave the Union. In
November of 1861, he was elected to the
Confederate congress.

Tyler went to Richmond to begin his work
in the congress. Soon after he arrived, he was
surprised to see Mrs. Tyler arrive at the hotel
where he was staying. She had planned to join
him there, but not for another week. Mrs.
Tyler told her husband about a terrible night-
mare she had had the night before. She
dreamed that he was very ill and needed her
help. Mrs. Tyler was so worried when she
awoke that she decided to leave for Richmond
at once. Tyler was pleased to see her, but he

▶ The Tylers had their seventh child when John was 70 years old.

▶ Tyler, Texas, officially became a town in 1847. It was named for President John Tyler.

refused to worry about her dream. The next morning, though, he felt quite ill. Within two days, he was dead. The Tyler family always believed that Julia's dream foresaw his death.

More than 150 carriages followed Tyler's coffin to the cemetery. He was buried next to the tomb of President James Monroe, the nation's fifth president.

Tyler was the only former president to join the Confederacy. For years after his death, the North considered him a traitor, someone who had betrayed his country. It was 53 years before the U.S. government put a memorial at his gravesite. Tyler probably would not have minded. Popularity was never important to him. To John Tyler, the most important thing was to do what he believed was right. He always stood up for his beliefs, even if they were unpopular.

In 1862, Tyler died from a stroke. He was 71 years old.

36

THE MANSION AT SHERWOOD FOREST WAS OLD WHEN JOHN TYLER BOUGHT it in 1842. People said it had been haunted for at least 50 years by the time he moved there with his family. And people say it has been haunted ever since. A ghost called the Gray Lady is said to roam the mansion.

Payne Tyler is married to John Tyler's grandson. She and her husband still live at Sherwood Forest and are among the many family members and visitors who have seen the ghost. She says, "It is thought that she was a governess, who had charge of a small child at one time here. She would take the child from a first floor bedroom and walk her up through the hidden staircase to a second floor nursery. There, she would rock the child on her lap in a rocking chair. She is definitely in the house. I know, because I have personally had encounters with her."

1790 John Tyler is born in Charles City County, Virginia, on March 29.

1802 Tyler begins classes at William and Mary College.

1807 Tyler graduates from William and Mary College. He begins to study law.

1809 Tyler passes his law exams. He moves to Richmond and works in the office of Edmund Randolph, who had been the nation's first attorney general.

1811 Tyler is elected to the Virginia House of Delegates. He holds this position until 1816.

1813 Tyler marries Letitia Christian on March 29, his 23rd birthday. They go on to have eight children.

1816 Tyler is elected to the U.S. House of Representatives. He holds the office from 1817 until 1821.

1818 General Andrew Jackson seizes East Florida without orders from the U.S. government. Although his actions are unconstitutional, many Americans consider him a hero. Tyler does not agree.

1823 Tyler takes office in the Virginia House of Delegates. He holds the position until 1825.

1825 Tyler is elected governor of Virginia. He holds the position for two terms.

1827 Tyler enters the U.S. Senate. He remains in office for nine years.

1828 Tyler supports Andrew Jackson in the presidential election because he has similar views about the Second Bank of the United States and states' rights. Jackson is elected president.

1833 Tyler opposes Jackson's Force Bill.

1834 Tyler and other senators censure Jackson's removal of government funds from the Second Bank of the United States.

1836 When the state of Virginia orders Tyler to cancel his censure of President Jackson, Tyler refuses and resigns his seat in the Senate. He quits the Democratic Party and joins the Whigs, a political party united by its opposition to Jackson.

1838 Tyler returns to the Virginia legislature for two years.

1839 Tyler is elected Speaker of the Virginia House of Delegates.

1840 The Whigs nominate William Henry Harrison as their presidential candidate and Tyler as the vice presidential candidate. They win the election.

1841 Tyler is vice president for only one month before William Henry Harrison dies on April 4. Tyler insists that the Constitution gives the vice president the full powers of the president if the president dies. Congress agrees, and Tyler takes the oath of office on April 9. All but one of Harrison's Whig cabinet members quit their jobs.

1842 The Webster-Ashburton Treaty settles the boundary dispute between Maine and Canada. Tyler promises to protect Hawaii from invasion by foreign powers. Letitia Christian Tyler dies on September 10 at the age of 51. She is the first wife of a president to die while her husband is in office. Whigs try unsuccessfully to impeach Tyler in the House of Representatives.

1843 Tyler begins secret meetings with Sam Houston, the president of Texas, hoping to finalize the annexation of Texas. They come to an agreement and sign a treaty. The Senate must support this act but refuses to do so.

1844 The treaty of Wang Hiya gives the U.S. access to Chinese ports. Tyler marries Julia Gardiner in June. Recognizing he has little chance to win the election, Tyler does not run for president. James K. Polk, who was strongly in favor of the annexation of Texas, wins the election.

1845 Congress agrees to the annexation of Texas. Tyler signs an act admitting it to the Union three days before he leaves office. He and Julia return to Virginia to live at their plantation, Sherwood Forest.

1860 Tyler is named the chancellor of the College of William and Mary.

1861 Tyler is named the chairman of the Peace Convention in Washington, D.C. Members of the convention try to reach a compromise to avoid a civil war. They are unable to reach an agreement, and war breaks out on April 12. Tyler is elected to the Congress of the Confederate States of America.

1862 Tyler dies in Richmond, Virginia, on January 18.

Glossary TERMS

annexation (an-ek-SAY-shun)
Annexation is the joining of something smaller (such as a territory) to something bigger (such as a country). Tyler was in favor of the annexation of Texas to the United States.

bill (BIL)
A bill is an idea for a new law that is presented to a group of lawmakers. Tyler vetoed many bills that were introduced by Congress.

cabinet (KAB-eh-net)
A cabinet is the group of people who advise a president. All but one member of Harrison's cabinet resigned shortly after Tyler took office.

candidate (KAN-duh-det)
A candidate is a person running in an election. The Whigs chose Tyler as their vice presidential candidate in 1840.

compromise (KOM-pruh-myz)
A compromise is a way to settle a disagreement in which both sides give up part of what they want. Tyler would not support the Missouri Compromise.

Confederate (kun-FED-ur-ut)
Confederate refers to the slave states (or the people who lived in those states) that left the Union in 1861. Tyler was elected to the Confederate congress.

constitution (kon-stih-TOO-shun)
A constitution is the set of basic principles that govern a state, country, or society. Tyler believed in the principles of the U.S. Constitution.

federal (FED-ur-ul)
Federal refers to the national government of the United States, rather than a state or city government. Tyler believed the states should have more power than the federal government.

frontier (frun-TEER)
A frontier is a region that is at the edge of or beyond settled land. The U.S. government gave public land to homesteaders on the frontier.

impeach (im-PEECH)
If the House of Representatives votes to impeach a president, it charges him or her with a crime or serious misdeed. Some congressmen wanted to impeach President Tyler.

inauguration (ih-nawg-yuh-RAY-shun)
An inauguration is the ceremony that takes place when a new president begins a term. The day of President Harrison's inauguration was cold and rainy.

legislature (LEJ-uh-slay-chur)
A legislature is the part of a government that makes laws. Tyler was elected to the Virginia state legislature.

pneumonia (noo-MOH-nyuh)
Pneumonia is a disease that causes swelling of the lungs, high fever, and difficulty breathing. President Harrison died from pneumonia.

**political party
(puh-LIT-uh-kul PAR-tee)**
A political party is a group of people who share similar ideas about how to run a government. Tyler joined the Democratic political party in 1827.

politics (PAWL-uh-tiks)
Politics refers to the actions and practices of the government. Tyler began his long career in politics with the Virginia state legislature.

principles (PRIN-suh-puls)
Principles are basic beliefs, or what people believe to be right and true. Tyler firmly believed in the principles of the Constitution.

statesmen (STAYTZ-men)
Statesmen are people skilled at managing public or national affairs. Tyler said he was glad to have able statesmen in his cabinet.

tariff (TAR-iff)
A tariff is a tax on goods brought in from other countries. Tyler vetoed a tariff bill in 1842.

territories (TAIR-ih-tor-eez)
Territories are lands or regions, especially lands that belong to a government. The U.S. government had to decide whether to allow slavery in its new territories.

treaty (TREE-tee)
A treaty is a formal agreement between nations. Tyler signed a treaty with the president of Texas in 1843.

**unconstitutional
(un-kon-stih-TOO-shuh-nel)**
Unconstitutional means going against the Constitution of the United States. Tyler opposed any law that he believed was unconstitutional.

union (YOON-yen)
A union is the joining together of two people or groups of people, such as states. The Union is another name for the United States.

veto (VEE-toh)
A veto is the president's power to refuse to sign a bill into law. Tyler vetoed bills that he did not like.

Our PRESIDENTS

President	Birthplace	Life Span	Presidency	Political Party	First Lady
George Washington	Virginia	1732–1799	1789–1797	None	Martha Dandridge Custis Washington
John Adams	Massachusetts	1735–1826	1797–1801	Federalist	Abigail Smith Adams
Thomas Jefferson	Virginia	1743–1826	1801–1809	Democratic-Republican	widower
James Madison	Virginia	1751–1836	1809–1817	Democratic Republican	Dolley Payne Todd Madison
James Monroe	Virginia	1758–1831	1817–1825	Democratic Republican	Elizabeth Kortright Monroe
John Quincy Adams	Massachusetts	1767–1848	1825–1829	Democratic-Republican	Louisa Johnson Adams
Andrew Jackson	South Carolina	1767–1845	1829–1837	Democrat	widower
Martin Van Buren	New York	1782–1862	1837–1841	Democrat	widower
William H. Harrison	Virginia	1773–1841	1841	Whig	Anna Symmes Harrison
John Tyler	Virginia	1790–1862	1841–1845	Whig	Letitia Christian Tyler / Julia Gardiner Tyler
James K. Polk	North Carolina	1795–1849	1845–1849	Democrat	Sarah Childress Polk

Our PRESIDENTS

President	Birthplace	Life Span	Presidency	Political Party	First Lady
Zachary Taylor	Virginia	1784–1850	1849–1850	Whig	Margaret Mackall Smith Taylor
Millard Fillmore	New York	1800–1874	1850–1853	Whig	Abigail Powers Fillmore
Franklin Pierce	New Hampshire	1804–1869	1853–1857	Democrat	Jane Means Appleton Pierce
James Buchanan	Pennsylvania	1791–1868	1857–1861	Democrat	never married
Abraham Lincoln	Kentucky	1809–1865	1861–1865	Republican	Mary Todd Lincoln
Andrew Johnson	North Carolina	1808–1875	1865–1869	Democrat	Eliza McCardle Johnson
Ulysses S. Grant	Ohio	1822–1885	1869–1877	Republican	Julia Dent Grant
Rutherford B. Hayes	Ohio	1822–1893	1877–1881	Republican	Lucy Webb Hayes
James A. Garfield	Ohio	1831–1881	1881	Republican	Lucretia Rudolph Garfield
Chester A. Arthur	Vermont	1829–1886	1881–1885	Republican	widower
Grover Cleveland	New Jersey	1837–1908	1885–1889	Democrat	Frances Folsom Cleveland

Our PRESIDENTS

President	Birthplace	Life Span	Presidency	Political Party	First Lady
Benjamin Harrison	Ohio	1833–1901	1889–1893	Republican	Caroline Scott Harrison
Grover Cleveland	New Jersey	1837–1908	1893–1897	Democrat	Frances Folsom Cleveland
William McKinley	Ohio	1843–1901	1897–1901	Republican	Ida Saxton McKinley
Theodore Roosevelt	New York	1858–1919	1901–1909	Republican	Edith Kermit Carow Roosevelt
William H. Taft	Ohio	1857–1930	1909–1913	Republican	Helen Herron Taft
Woodrow Wilson	Virginia	1856–1924	1913–1921	Democrat	Ellen L. Axson Wilson Edith Bolling Galt Wilson
Warren G. Harding	Ohio	1865–1923	1921–1923	Republican	Florence Kling De Wolfe Harding
Calvin Coolidge	Vermont	1872–1933	1923–1929	Republican	Grace Goodhue Coolidge
Herbert C. Hoover	Iowa	1874–1964	1929–1933	Republican	Lou Henry Hoover
Franklin D. Roosevelt	New York	1882–1945	1933–1945	Democrat	Anna Eleanor Roosevelt Roosevelt
Harry S. Truman	Missouri	1884–1972	1945–1953	Democrat	Elizabeth Wallace Truman

Our PRESIDENTS

President	Birthplace	Life Span	Presidency	Political Party	First Lady
Dwight D. Eisenhower	Texas	1890–1969	1953–1961	Republican	Mary "Mamie" Doud Eisenhower
John F. Kennedy	Massachusetts	1917–1963	1961–1963	Democrat	Jacqueline Bouvier Kennedy
Lyndon B. Johnson	Texas	1908–1973	1963–1969	Democrat	Claudia Alta Taylor Johnson
Richard M. Nixon	California	1913–1994	1969–1974	Republican	Thelma Catherine Ryan Nixon
Gerald Ford	Nebraska	1913–	1974–1977	Republican	Elizabeth "Betty" Bloomer Warren Ford
James Carter	Georgia	1924–	1977–1981	Democrat	Rosalynn Smith Carter
Ronald Reagan	Illinois	1911–	1981–1989	Republican	Nancy Davis Reagan
George Bush	Massachusetts	1924–	1989–1993	Republican	Barbara Pierce Bush
William Clinton	Arkansas	1946–	1993–2001	Democrat	Hillary Rodham Clinton
George W. Bush	Connecticut	1946–	2001–	Republican	Laura Welch Bush

Presidential FACTS

Qualifications

To run for president, a candidate must

- be at least 35 years old
- be a citizen who was born in the United States
- have lived in the United States for 14 years

Term of Office

A president's term of office is four years. No president can stay in office for more than two terms.

Election Date

The presidential election takes place every four years on the first Tuesday of November.

Inauguration Date

Presidents are inaugurated on January 20.

Oath of Office

I do solemnly swear I will faithfully execute the office of the President of the United States and will to the best of my ability preserve, protect, and defend the Constitution of the United States.

Write a Letter to the President

One of the best things about being a U.S. citizen is that Americans get to participate in their government. They can speak out if they feel government leaders aren't doing their jobs. They can also praise leaders who are going the extra mile. Do you have something you'd like the president to do? Should the president worry more about the environment and encourage people to recycle? Should the government spend more money on our schools? You can write a letter to the president to say how you feel!

1600 Pennsylvania Avenue
Washington, D.C. 20500

You can even send an e-mail to: president@whitehouse.gov

For Further INFORMATION

Internet Sites

Visit Sherwood Forest, President Tyler's home:
http://www.sherwoodforest.org/index.html

Locate a list of Web links relating to Tyler:
http://www.geocities.com/CapitolHill/Lobby/5296/pres_john_tyler.html

Search topics related to the presidency and learn more about the U.S. government:
http://www.netcolony.com/news/presidents/

Learn more about all the presidents and visit the White House:
http://www.whitehouse.gov/WH/glimpse/presidents/html/presidents.html
http://www.thepresidency.org/presinfo.htm
http://www.americanpresidents.org/

Books

Feinberg, Barbara Silberdick. *America's First Ladies.* New York: Franklin Watts, 1998.

Gaines, Ann Graham. *William Henry Harrison: Our Ninth President.* Chanhassen, MN: The Child's World, 2002.

Hakim, Joy. *From Colonies to Country.* New York: Oxford University Press, 1993.

Hakim, Joy. *Liberty for All?* New York: Oxford University Press, 1994.

Rubel, David. *The United States in the 19th Century.* New York: Scholastic, 1996.

Toynton, Evelyn. *Growing up in America.* Brookfield, CT: Millbrook Press, 1995.

Index